How Should I Approach Suffering?

Crucial Questions booklets provide a quick introduction to definitive Christian truths. This expanding collection includes titles such as:

Who Is Jesus?

Can I Trust the Bible?

Does Prayer Change Things?

Can I Know God's Will?

How Should I Live in This World?

What Does It Mean to Be Born Again?

Can I Be Sure I'm Saved?

What Is Faith?

What Can I Do with My Guilt?

What Is the Trinity?

CQ

How Should I Approach Suffering?

R.C. SPROUL

Ligonier Ministries

How Should I Approach Suffering?

Adapted from *Surprised by Suffering* (1988, 2009 by R.C. Sproul) and *Dealing with Difficult Problems* (2012 by R.C. Sproul).

Published by Ligonier Ministries
421 Ligonier Court, Sanford, FL 32771
Ligonier.org

Printed in China
Amity Printing Company
0000225
First edition

ISBN 978-1-64289-668-8 (Paperback)
ISBN 978-1-64289-669-5 (ePub)

Cover design: Ligonier Creative
Interior design and typeset: Katherine Lloyd, The DESK

Library of Congress Control Number: 2024945858

Contents

Chapter One

Suffering, Perplexity, and Despair

Christians are those who have faith in Christ. We all aspire to possess a faith that is strong and enduring. The reality, however, is that faith is not a constant thing. Our faith wavers between moments of supreme exultation and trying times that push us to the rim of despair. Doubt rises up in us and threatens our peace. Rare is the saint who has a tranquil spirit in all seasons.

Suffering is one of the most significant challenges to any believer's faith. When pain, grief, persecution, or other forms of suffering strike, we find ourselves caught off guard, confused, and full of questions. Suffering can strain faith to the limits.

Paul wrote poignantly about his own struggles in times of distress: "We are hard pressed on every side, yet not crushed; we are perplexed, but not in despair; persecuted, but not forsaken; struck down, but not destroyed—always carrying about in the body the dying of the Lord Jesus, that the life of Jesus also may be manifested in our body" (2 Cor. 4:8–10, NKJV).

The Apostle said that he was "hard pressed on every side, yet not crushed." He made no attempt to mask his pain in a fraudulent piety. The Christian is not a Stoic. Neither does he flee into a fantasy world that denies the reality of suffering. Paul freely admitted the pressure he experienced.

We all know what it means to be hard pressed. We use the word *pressure* to describe tense moments in our lives. Troubles in our jobs, troubles in our marriages, and troubles in our relationships can mount up and attack our spirits. If we add the tragic death of a loved one or the difficulty of a prolonged illness to these daily pressures, we feel the pain of being hard pressed all the more.

To be hard pressed is to feel as though we are used automobiles that have been consigned to the junk heap and put in a metal compactor. To be hard pressed is to feel a massive weight that threatens to crush us.

When we experience severe heartbreak, we may be inclined to say, "I'm crushed." But this is hyperbole. We may feel crushed; we may even come close to being crushed. But the bold declaration of the Apostle is that we are *not* crushed.

God knows our limits far better than we do. In one respect, we are very much like camels. When a camel's load is heavy, it doesn't ask its master for more weight. Its knees get a bit wobbly and it groans beneath the burden, but it can take on more before its back will break. The promise of God is not that He will never give us more weight than we *want* to carry. The promise of God is that He will never put more on us than we *can* bear.

Note that Paul did not say, "We are *lightly* pressed on every side." He said that we are *hard* pressed. At first glance, these words seem in direct conflict with the promises of Christ. Jesus said: "Come to me, all who labor and are heavy laden, and I will give you rest. Take my yoke upon you, and learn from me, for I am gentle and lowly in heart, and you will find rest for your souls. For my yoke is easy, and my burden is light" (Matt. 11:28–30).

It may not always seem to us that the burden Christ gives us is light. With these words, it almost seems as though Jesus approaches us under false pretenses. But His words are true. He *does* give rest to those who are heavy laden. The words *easy* and *light* are relative terms. *Easy* is relative to a standard of difficulty. *Light* is relative to a standard of heaviness. What is difficult to bear without Christ is made far more bearable with Christ. What is a heavy burden to carry alone becomes a far lighter burden to carry with His help.

It is precisely the presence and help of Christ in times of suffering that makes it possible for us to stand up under pressure. It was because of Christ that Paul could triumphantly declare that though he was hard pressed, he was not crushed. We may feel like junked automobiles in a metal compactor, but Christ stands as a shield to prevent the pressure that comes on us from crushing us entirely.

To suffer without Christ is to risk being totally and completely crushed. I've often wondered how people cope with the trials of life without the strength found in Him. His presence and comfort are so vital that I'm not surprised when unbelievers accuse Christians of using religion as a crutch. We remember Karl Marx's charge that "religion is the opiate of the people." He saw religious belief as something that is used for dulling the effects of pain. Others have charged that religion is a bromide used by the weak in times of trouble.

It is no shame to call on God for help in times of trouble. It is His delight to minister to us in our time of pain. There is no scandal in the mercy of God to the afflicted. He is like a father who pities his children and moves to comfort them when they are hurting. To suffer without the comfort of God is no virtue. To lean on His comfort is no vice, contrary to Marx.

Paul added, "We are perplexed, but not in despair." Perplexity often accompanies suffering. When we are stricken with illness or grief, we are often bewildered and confused. Our first question is "Why?" We ask, "Why would God allow this to happen to me?"

Scripture admonishes us *not* to think that it is a strange or unusual thing that we should suffer. Peter wrote: "Beloved, do not be surprised at the fiery trial when it comes upon you to test you, as though something strange were happening to you. But rejoice insofar as you share

Christ's sufferings, that you may also rejoice and be glad" (1 Peter 4:12–13). These words echo Paul's statement about "filling up what is lacking" in the sufferings of Christ (Col. 1:24), a curious affirmation that we will look at more closely in chapters 2 and 4.

Peter adds these words: "But let none of you suffer as a murderer or a thief or an evildoer or as a meddler. Yet if anyone suffers as a Christian, let him not be ashamed, but let him glorify God in that name" (1 Peter 4:15–16). When the criminal suffers for his crime, he may be distressed, but he has no reason to be perplexed. There is no surprise that punishment should be the consequence of crime. There is shame attached to this sort of suffering.

To suffer as a Christian carries no shame. Peter concludes: "Therefore let those who suffer according to God's will entrust their souls to a faithful Creator while doing good" (v. 19). Here Peter erases all doubt about the question whether it is ever the will of God that we should suffer. He speaks of those who suffer "according to God's will." This text means that suffering itself is part of the sovereign will of God.

Earlier in his epistle, Peter spoke of the fruit of our suffering:

> In this you rejoice, though now for a little while, if necessary, you have been grieved by various trials, so that the tested genuineness of your faith—more precious than gold that perishes though it is tested by fire—may be found to result in praise and glory and honor at the revelation of Jesus Christ. Though you have not seen him, you love him. Though you do not now see him, you believe in him and rejoice with joy that is inexpressible and filled with glory, obtaining the outcome of your faith, the salvation of your souls. (1:6–9)

This passage shows how it is possible to be perplexed but not in despair. Our suffering has a purpose—it helps us toward the end of our faith, which is the salvation of our souls. Suffering is a crucible. As gold is refined in the fire, purged of its dross and impurities, so our faith is tested by fire. Gold perishes. Our souls do not. We experience pain and grief for a season. It is while we are in the fire that perplexity assails us. But there is another side to the fire. As the dross burns away, the genuineness of faith is purified unto the salvation of our souls.

It is when we view our suffering as meaningless—without

purpose—that we are tempted to despair. A woman who endures the travail of childbirth is able to do so because she knows that the end result will be a new life. But not all of those who are terminally ill have the same hope of a good result as those giving birth to a child. If death is the end, the suffering that attends it *should* drive us to full and final despair.

The message of Christ, however, is that death is not unto death but unto life. So the analogy of childbirth applies. In fact, it is used to describe the suffering of Christ and of the whole creation. Isaiah wrote, "Out of the anguish of his soul he shall see and be satisfied" (Isa. 53:11). Likewise, Paul told us: "For we know that the whole creation has been groaning together in the pains of childbirth until now. And not only the creation, but we ourselves, who have the firstfruits of the Spirit, groan inwardly as we wait eagerly for adoption as sons, the redemption of our bodies" (Rom. 8:22–23).

We may be perplexed, but we should not despair. The pain of suffering in itself would be enough to drive us to despair were we not persuaded of the redemption that lies before us.

Still, even that redemption is not always enough to keep us from approaching the rim of despair. Scripture repeatedly reveals the struggles of the greatest saints with the problem of despair. More than one biblical figure cursed the day of his birth and pleaded for the privilege of death.

Moses faced the dark night of the soul when he cried out to God: "If you will treat me like this, kill me at once, if I find favor in your sight, that I may not see my wretchedness" (Num. 11:15). Job cursed the day of his birth: "Why did I not die at birth, come out from the womb and expire? Why did the knees receive me? Or why the breasts, that I should nurse? For then I would have lain down and been quiet; I would have slept; then I would have been at rest" (Job 3:11–13). Jeremiah expressed the same sentiment: "Cursed be the day on which I was born! The day when my mother bore me, let it not be blessed! Cursed be the man who brought the news to my father, 'A son is born to you,' making him very glad. . . . Why did I come out from the womb to see toil and sorrow, and spend my days in shame?" (Jer. 20:14–15, 18).

It is when suffering lingers that we are pushed to these depths. The Danish philosopher Søren Kierkegaard once remarked that one of the worst situations a human being can face is to want to die and not be allowed to do so. The deep desire to be released from suffering lies at the core of the issue of euthanasia. It is argued that we are more humane to animals than we are to people. We shoot horses and we put our dogs to sleep, but we maintain human life as long as possible.

Historically, both the church and the medical profession (following the Hippocratic oath) have followed the maxim that we ought to do everything possible to sustain life. But with the advent of modern techniques, it is now possible to keep people technically alive beyond the scope of any possible hope for recovery. Thus, modern technology has introduced severe moral dilemmas into the matter of dying.

It must be said that God does not permit us to commit suicide. Suicide, in its fullest expression, involves a surrender to despair. (This does not mean that suicide is the unpardonable sin. People commit suicide for all sorts of reasons and in all sorts of conditions. We don't really know the state of mind that people are in when they do it. We leave the question of the fate of suicide victims to the mercy of God.) Whatever the complexities of suffering, we know that we are not given suicide as an option for death.

The only way to avoid despair is to place our faith in Jesus Christ for the salvation that God provides. David summed up the matter: "I believe that I shall look upon the goodness of the Lord in the land of the living!" (Ps. 27:13). Likewise, the Apostle Paul, in the same epistle in which he said, "We are perplexed, but not in despair," also wrote:

> For we do not want you to be unaware, brothers, of the affliction we experienced in Asia. For we were so utterly burdened beyond our strength that we despaired of life itself. Indeed, we felt that we had received the sentence of death. But that was to make us rely not on ourselves but on God who raises the dead. He delivered us from such a deadly peril, and he will deliver us. On him we have set our hope that he will deliver us again. (2 Cor. 1:8–10)

Paul entered into despair. But his despair was limited. It was not ultimate despair. He despaired of his earthly life. He was sure that he was going to die, but Paul did not despair of the ultimate deliverance from death. He knew the promise of Christ for victory over death.

Chapter Two

Understanding Suffering

In Luke 13:1–5, we read this account:

> There were some present at that very time who told [Jesus] about the Galileans whose blood Pilate had mingled with their sacrifices. And he answered them, "Do you think that these Galileans were worse sinners than all the other Galileans, because they suffered in this way? No, I tell you; but unless you repent, you will all likewise perish. Or those

> eighteen on whom the tower in Siloam fell and killed them: do you think that they were worse offenders than all the others who lived in Jerusalem? No, I tell you; but unless you repent, you will all likewise perish."

People came to Jesus and asked, basically: "How could God allow these things to happen? If God is good, how could He stand by and let the tower fall on the heads of innocent people just minding their business, walking down the street? Or allow them to become victims of this savage attack of Pilate's forces? He mixed the blood of the people with the sacrifices."

We're surprised when these things happen. And we may be even more surprised at Jesus' response: "If you think that these things happened to these people because they were worse sinners than anybody else, I tell you, no. But unless you repent, you will likewise perish."

What's our Lord saying here? I think what He is telling His inquirers is this: "You're asking Me the wrong question. The question you should be asking is: 'Why didn't that temple fall on my head? Why wasn't my blood mixed with the blood of the sacrifices with the Galileans?'" Somehow, we assume that God owes it to us to give us a life free of suffering.

We have to be careful when we look at the whole question of suffering. To ask the question "Why?," when we're earnestly seeking an answer, is a legitimate thing, but the question "Why?" can be a thinly veiled accusation.

We need to keep that in front of us at all times. The reality of suffering is something that we all have to deal with—and we deal with it in a pagan world. Part of the difficulty that we experience in dealing with this particular problem is that so often, we hear views of pain and suffering that are pagan views. We need to understand the difference between the Christian understanding of suffering and pagan views of suffering. Three different views of suffering have been popular at one time or another in the pagan world.

The first is the docetic view: that suffering and pain are an illusion. This view is basically one of denial. It says that suffering is just a matter of the mind; it's not real, and we need to understand that it's simply an illusion. In reality, saying that suffering is not real has little value to somebody on a hospital bed, because we all know that it is real. There is such a thing as pain; there is such a thing as sorrow. And denying the reality of it is no solution to the problem.

A second way that pagans have dealt with the problem of suffering and evil is found in what I call the historic or classic Stoic view. You hear the axioms of Stoicism creeping into our popular culture when you hear such statements as "Keep a stiff upper lip" and "Don't let anything get you down." The Stoics believed that we live in a world that is controlled by material forces. And these material forces operate according to fixed, deterministic laws, and we have absolutely no control over what happens to us in this environment. That which happens to us is our fate. It is the result of impersonal forces, and we have no freedom to determine our own destiny.

The only way that we do have the ability to exercise our freedom and to affect the state of our existence is by directing our attitudes or our emotions with respect to things that befall us. The Stoics sought to practice diligently the art of imperturbability. That is, you practice controlling your emotions to such a degree that nothing will perturb you; nothing will upset you.

The third way that pagans have sought to deal with suffering historically is through a method expounded by the Stoics' chief rivals in their day, the hedonists. Hedonism, historically, describes or defines the good in terms of the elimination of pain and the acquisition of pleasure.

In the ancient world, there were two different types of hedonists in their philosophical orientation, one that I will call the crass hedonists, and the other that I'll call the more refined hedonists. The crass hedonists were called the Cyrenaics, and the Cyrenaics were crude in their pursuit of pleasure.

They lived lives of unbridled licentiousness, indulging in as much sex and drink and food and other sensuous pleasure that they could. That was their way to happiness. But again, this crass school of hedonists was short-lived because it didn't take them long to figure out that if you have an unbridled appetite for pleasure that has no moderation or no balance, the pain of the consequences of such unbridled self-indulgence will be felt very shortly and acutely.

So a new version of hedonism was developed in a more refined, sophisticated way by those who were called the Epicureans. They sought not maximum pleasure but optimum pleasure. They sought the most amount of pleasure that one could have without at the same time increasing the threshold of pain.

Hedonism, in either its crude form or its refined form, still attracts people today. We still have Epicureans, and we have a culture that has been drenched and saturated in the philosophy of hedonism.

It's not an accident that suicide is the leading cause of death among certain age groups in this nation, because people are now taught that they have emerged from the slime; they're cosmic accidents; their lives are meaningless. Their suffering is therefore meaningless, and so they try to dull the pain and the ache of the anxiety of being hurled into a meaningless existence by seeking relief in the stupor of pleasure.

Nothing is new about that; it's just that the dimensions are different. Paul, when he addressed the Corinthians and gave his magnificent defense of the resurrection, stated at one point, "If the dead are not raised, 'Let us eat and drink, for tomorrow we die'" (1 Cor. 15:32).

This approach to hedonism, in many ways, is motivated by a fear of suffering and a desire to escape it. We talk of those who drown their sorrows in a bottle, and perhaps the most popular psychoanalysts in our culture are the bartenders who are found in every barroom in metropolitan areas, because a lot of people are unhappy, are suffering, and are in pain, desperately trying to find solace and relief from their pain in any way that they can.

These are just some of the ways that people cope with the reality of pain and suffering. Clearly, the biblical view of suffering stands in sharp contrast to these views, because the one overarching principle of the biblical view of suffering is this: Suffering, for the Christian, is never an exercise in futility. Suffering is used by God for redemptive purposes among His people, and we are told where to put our locus of astonishment. We are told by Peter and James that we ought not to think that it is something strange when we are called on to suffer, because the Christian faith is born in suffering. The way of salvation is the *Via Dolorosa*, the way of sadness, the way of the cross.

Christ Himself promises His people that they will have tribulation. They will have afflictions. Paul declares that he fills up in his own body the afflictions that have not yet been completed in the body of Christ, His church (Col. 1:24). We all are called to participate in the sorrows of Christ, who was called a man of sorrows and acquainted with grief (Isa. 53:3). And there's a difference between that and Stoicism.

Jesus was a man of sorrows, acquainted with grief. The Scriptures make it plain that grief is a legitimate human emotion, and there is nothing sinful about mourning the loss of a loved one. That emotion of grief, the emotion of sorrow, in and of itself is perfectly legitimate. It can easily become a spirit of self-pity or of bitterness, but those are distortions of legitimate emotions.

A legitimate emotion of sadness and sorrow not only is permitted by Scripture but in many cases is commended. We are told in the Old Testament that it is better to go to the house of mourning than to spend your time with fools.

When Paul speaks of the great benefit of our justification, whereby we're adopted into fellowship in the family of God, he says that being justified means that we have peace with God and access into His presence. He goes on to insist, "Not only that, but we rejoice in our sufferings, knowing that suffering produces endurance, and endurance produces character, and character produces hope, and hope does not put us to shame" (Rom. 5:3–5).

God uses tribulation, He uses our pain, not simply to punish us but to polish us, to sanctify us. In many cases, we go into the refiner's fire so that God will remove the dross from our life, draw us close to Himself, and, in the process of pain and suffering, make us more like Christ.

Paul then reminds us that the sufferings of this present time are but for a moment. They are not the final answer, and the sufferings that we are called to endure in this world aren't worthy to be compared with the glorious things that God has stored up in heaven for those who love Him.

In one sense, our suffering becomes a bridge to glory. That doesn't mean that we are supposed to go out and look for suffering and to say, "Thank You, Lord," every time the sky falls on our heads. Some people try to do that, and it can be a form of denial. It can be more docetic than it is Christian.

God doesn't promise that we will never go through the valley of the shadow of death. What He does promise us is that He will go with us. "Even though I walk through the valley of the shadow of death, I will fear no evil, for you are with me; your rod and your staff, they comfort me" (Ps. 23:4). We have the Good Shepherd. We have His presence. We have His consolation. That doesn't mean that we're removed from the arena of pain, but it means that we are upheld in the arena of pain.

Chapter Three

How to Deal with Anxiety

What negative prohibition did Jesus utter most frequently? The answer is simple, because this particular commandment was uttered so many times by Jesus that it was far ahead of whatever is in second place. It was this: "Fear not." In fact, Jesus says this so often that at times we miss its significance. I suspect that the reason that Jesus says this so often has something to do with His intimate knowledge and understanding of the frailty of our human makeup. We as a people tend to be fearful. We tend to struggle with anxiety.

In the Sermon on the Mount, we read these words from Jesus:

> "Therefore I tell you, do not be anxious about your life, what you will eat or what you will drink, nor about your body, what you will put on. Is not life more than food, and the body more than clothing? Look at the birds of the air: they neither sow nor reap nor gather into barns, and yet your heavenly Father feeds them. Are you not of more value than they? And which of you by being anxious can add a single hour to his span of life? And why are you anxious about clothing? Consider the lilies of the field, how they grow: they neither toil nor spin, yet I tell you, even Solomon in all his glory was not arrayed like one of these. But if God so clothes the grass of the field, which today is alive and tomorrow is thrown into the oven, will he not much more clothe you, O you of little faith? Therefore do not be anxious, saying, 'What shall we eat?' or 'What shall we drink?' or 'What shall we wear?' For the Gentiles seek after all these things, and your heavenly Father knows that you need them all. But seek first the

> kingdom of God and his righteousness, and all these things will be added to you.
>
> "Therefore do not be anxious about tomorrow, for tomorrow will be anxious for itself. Sufficient for the day is its own trouble." (Matt. 6:25–34)

Jesus is not prohibiting careful planning or provision. He's saying: "Don't worry about tomorrow. You do what you have to do, but at the same time, tomorrow is in the hands of God." It really is our fear of the future more than anything else that drives anxieties and fears and worries. We don't ever worry about what happened yesterday. We don't have to worry about what happened yesterday, because yesterday is over. The focal point of our worries is always the future. It's always about what has not yet taken place.

Jesus says not to be anxious, and then He rebukes His hearers for being of little faith because of their worries. Why does He do that? After all, there are fearful things out there. There are painful things that we may experience. And not all of our worries go unrealized. At the same time, we are told that the coward dies a thousand times, but the courageous person only once. The coward goes through the experience by worrying about it many times before the actual occurrence takes place.

So this comes down to the relationship between our fears of the future and faith. Our worries and anxieties really do come from a lack of trust in the promises of God. We all have faith, but our faith is limited, and sometimes our faith does not get us past the anxiety of what will happen, because we're afraid that God will not do what He promises to do. To be a Christian is to trust God for your entire life. The greatest way to do that is to immerse ourselves in the Word of God, because nothing dispels fear more quickly than the reinforcement and our understanding of the promises of God and the knowledge of the presence of God.

We may distinguish between three types of fear. The first is an objective, specific fear, such as a phobia. This might be a fear of small spaces or public speaking, dying or pain, or the dentist or snakes. These are specific fears, and there are specific ways to deal with them. We might do our best to avoid situations involving the things that we're afraid of, or we might employ coping strategies to deal with our fear.

The second kind of fear is what existentialist philosophers call *angst*—a nameless fear. You may have experienced this at some point: you're pacing around, your stomach is flip-flopping, your hands are shaking, you know that you're scared, you may be having an anxiety attack, and you have no idea why.

This nameless anxiety is often rooted in an even deeper fear. Again, it's the fear of the future. The existentialist philosophers have no optimism about what tomorrow will bring. In existentialism, man feels as though he's been hurled into a chaotic world. He has no meaningful beginning. He has emerged from the slime, and he is moving every moment toward annihilation. In this view, we are suspended between birth and death in a vortex of meaninglessness. That's always eating away at us.

From a Christian perspective, this nameless anxiety may be more deeply rooted in the third kind of fear, which is restlessness. Augustine of Hippo addressed this in his *Confessions* when he wrote, "Oh, Lord, Thou hast made us for Thyself, and our hearts are restless until they find their rest in Thee."

The only way I know of to get over this is to turn again to Jesus and rest in the peace that He provides. He said: "Peace I leave with you; my peace I give to you. Not as the world gives do I give to you. Let not your hearts be troubled, neither let them be afraid" (John 14:27). The peace that Jesus is talking about here is the opposite of restlessness. It is a calmness of spirit that comes when you are in fellowship with God, and you can trust Him for tomorrow. He is the One who conquers fear.

Chapter Four

Walking the *Via Dolorosa*

Our Savior was a suffering Savior. He went before us into the uncharted land of agony and death. He went where no man is called to go. His Father gave Him a cup to drink that will never touch our lips. God will not ask us to endure anything comparable to the distress that Christ took on Himself. Wherever God calls us to go, whatever He summons us to endure, will fall far short of what Jesus experienced.

From the beginning of His ministry, Jesus was conscious of His mission. He knew that He was under a death sentence. He bore in His body the ravages of every evil, every sickness, and every pain known to the human race. Jesus suffered so deeply because the extent of evil in the world is so vast. Every consequence of every sin of each one of His people was placed on Him on the cross. To carry this dreadful burden was His vocation. To bear this pain and disease was His mission. The magnitude of this horror is beyond our understanding, but He understood it because it was His to bear.

Jesus endured His suffering to redeem His people. But those He redeemed are not thereby delivered from all pain and misery. Indeed, as we will see, we His people are called to participate in His suffering.

The idea that the Son of God would come in the flesh and suffer was unthinkable to many of His contemporaries. The scandalous news of the New Testament is that God became incarnate. The eternal, divine Word was made flesh. That flesh was vulnerable to all physical torment.

The Greeks' idea of God was so spiritual, so ethereal, that they did not even have room for the concept of incarnation. In their view, God could never be involved with physical suffering simply because God could never be involved with anything physical.

The Jews could accept the idea that God could appear in human form, but that God in human flesh could actually suffer was beyond their comprehension.

After the moment of Peter's great confession of the Christ at Caesarea Philippi came one of the sharpest rebukes he ever heard from Jesus. It all began with Peter's answer to Jesus' question, "Who do you say that I am?" (Matt. 16:15). Peter replied, "You are the Christ, the Son of the living God" (v. 16). For this response, Peter received the benediction of Jesus: "Blessed are you, Simon Bar-Jonah! For flesh and blood has not revealed this to you, but my Father who is in heaven. And I tell you, you are Peter, and on this rock I will build my church, and the gates of hell shall not prevail against it" (vv. 17–18). What higher commendation could a man receive than this blessing from Christ Himself?

Moments later, however, this same man received a stinging rebuke from Jesus: "Get behind me, Satan! You are a hindrance to me. For you are not setting your mind on the things of God, but on the things of man" (v. 23). These words were spoken not to Satan but to Peter. The dialogue here is volatile. One moment Jesus put His benediction on Peter and the next moment He called him "Satan." How can we explain this dramatic shift in tone and words? Jesus was not given to undue severity in His treatment of people. Neither was He two-faced, praising with one side of His mouth and cursing with the other.

This shift of speech must be understood in light of the interval that passed between the commendation and the rebuke. The interval contained an exchange between Peter and Jesus regarding suffering: "From that time Jesus began to show his disciples that he must go to Jerusalem and suffer many things from the elders and chief priests and scribes, and be killed, and on the third day be raised" (v. 21).

Jesus was showing that He must suffer and die. His journey to Jerusalem was not optional. He had a destiny to fulfill, a rendezvous on Golgotha. This "mustness" was rooted in His vocation. He was called to perform a task. It was His duty to suffer and die.

It was precisely at this point of duty that Peter challenged Him: "And Peter took him aside and began to rebuke him, saying, 'Far be it from you, Lord! This shall never happen to you'" (v. 22). At least Peter had the grace to rebuke his Lord privately. He didn't flaunt his arrogance publicly, though the Holy Spirit entered his unspeakable presumption in the record of Scripture.

Peter demanded that Jesus distance Himself from suffering and death. He wanted the kingdom to come in the way that he thought fitting rather than God's way. God's way was the way of the cross, the *Via Dolorosa*. Jesus recognized in Peter's demand the same seductive suggestion that Satan had offered in the wilderness.

Theologians argue about when in Jesus' life it entered His consciousness that He must suffer and die, but the Bible makes it clear that the idea of the suffering Messiah was formulated long before Caesarea Philippi. The concept was foreshadowed as early as Genesis 3:15: "I will put enmity between you and the woman, and between your offspring and her offspring; he shall bruise your head, and you shall bruise his heel." This is the *protoeuangelion*, the first hint of the gospel that was to come. Later, the idea was greatly expanded in the Suffering Servant motif of Isaiah.

In the garden of Gethsemane, Jesus entered into His sorrow. He said to His disciples: "My soul is very sorrowful, even to death; remain here, and watch with me" (Matt. 26:38). The Scriptures tell us that after saying these words, Jesus went farther into the olive grove and fell on His face as He prayed: "My Father, if it be possible, let this cup pass from me; nevertheless, not as I will, but as you will" (v. 39). Luke adds to the historical record these words: "And being in agony he prayed more earnestly; and his sweat became like great drops of blood falling down to the ground" (Luke 22:44).

Never did a man pray more earnestly than Christ prayed in Gethsemane. Who will charge Jesus with failure to pray in faith? He put His request before the Father with sweat like blood: "Take this cup away from Me." This prayer was straightforward and without ambiguity—Jesus was crying out for relief. He asked for the horribly bitter cup to be removed. Every ounce of His humanity shrank from the cup. He begged the Father to relieve Him of His duty.

But God said no. The way of suffering was the Father's plan. It was the Father's will. The cross was not Satan's idea. The passion of Christ was not the result of human contingency. It was not the accidental contrivance of Caiaphas, Herod, or Pilate. The cup was prepared, delivered, and administered by almighty God.

Jesus qualified His prayer: "If it is Your will . . ." Jesus did not "name it and claim it." He knew His Father well enough to understand that it might not be His will to remove the cup. So the story does not end with the words "And the Father repented of the evil He had planned, removed the cup, and caused Jesus to live happily ever after." Such words border on blasphemy. The gospel is not a fairy tale. The Father would not negotiate the cup. Jesus was called to drink it to its last dregs. And He accepted it: "Nevertheless, not my will, but yours, be done" (Luke 22:42).

This "nevertheless" was the supreme prayer of faith. The prayer of faith is not a demand that we place on God. It is not a presumption of a granted request. The authentic prayer of faith is one that models Jesus' prayer. It is always uttered in a spirit of subordination. In all our prayers, we must let God be God. Prayers are always to be requests made in humility and submission to the Father's will.

Though the text is not explicit, it is clear that Jesus left the garden with the Father's answer to His plea. There was no cursing or bitterness. His meat and His drink were to do the Father's will. Once the Father said no, it was settled. Jesus prepared Himself for the cross.

In the life and passion of Christ, we see most clearly that suffering is the way God has chosen to bring redemption to a fallen world. Jesus was known as a man of sorrows, one who was acquainted with grief (Isa. 53:3). His life and ministry followed in detail the mission of the Suffering Servant of the Lord set forth by the prophet Isaiah.

That the New Testament identifies Jesus with the Suffering Servant of Israel matters profoundly. In the first place, our understanding of Jesus is tied to this question. I do not think it is an overstatement to declare that the New Testament portrait of Jesus stands or falls with this issue. The agonizing question of the meaning of our own suffering is tied to it as well.

In modern times, we have seen a kind of biblical scholarship that considers all references by Jesus to Isaiah's Suffering Servant prophecies as inventions of the New Testament writers. The theory holds that after Jesus went through His passion, the leaders of the early church had to invent an explanation for all His suffering. Therefore, they created this link between Isaiah's Suffering Servant and Jesus. Then they put words into Jesus' mouth that He never uttered.

The critics have self-interested reasons to reject the biblical view of Christ. Yet if we know anything of the historical Jesus, we know Him as One who suffered and died as the Servant of God. Luke's gospel records these words of Jesus: "For I tell you that this Scripture must be fulfilled in me: 'And he was numbered with the transgressors.' For what is written about me has its fulfillment" (Luke 22:37).

Here Jesus quoted directly from Isaiah 53. He identified Himself with the Suffering Servant of God. The nation of Israel was called to be a suffering servant. That vocation was then personalized and crystallized in one man, who represented Israel. Jesus suffered for us. Yet we are called to participate in His suffering. Though He was uniquely the fulfillment of Isaiah's prophecy, there is still an application of this vocation for us. We are given both the duty and the privilege to participate in the suffering of Christ.

A mysterious reference to this idea is found in the writings of the Apostle Paul: "Now I rejoice in my sufferings for your sake, and in my flesh I am filling up what is lacking in Christ's afflictions for the sake of his body, that is, the church" (Col. 1:24). Here Paul declared that he rejoiced in his suffering. Surely he did not mean that he enjoyed pain and affliction. Rather, the cause of his joy was found in the meaning of his suffering. He said that he filled up "what is lacking in Christ's afflictions."

On the surface, Paul's statement is astonishing. What could possibly have been lacking in the afflictions of Christ? Did Christ only half-finish His redemptive work, leaving it to Paul to complete it? Was Jesus overstating the case when He cried from the cross, "It is finished"

(John 19:30)? What exactly was lacking in the suffering of Christ?

In terms of the *value* of Jesus' suffering, it is blasphemous to suggest that anything was lacking. The merit of His atoning sacrifice is infinite. Nothing could possibly be added to His perfect obedience to make it even more perfect.

The answer to this difficult question lies in the broader teaching of the New Testament in regard to the believer's call to participate in the humiliation of Christ. Our baptism signifies that we are buried with Christ. Paul repeatedly pointed out that unless we are willing to participate in the humiliation of Jesus, we will not participate in His exaltation (see 2 Tim. 2:11–12).

Paul rejoiced that his suffering was a benefit to the church. The church is called to imitate Christ. It is called to walk the *Via Dolorosa*. Paul's favorite image for the church was a human body. The church is called the body of Christ. The church is really the mystical body of Christ on earth.

Christ so linked His church to Himself that when He first called Paul on the Damascus road, He said, "Saul, Saul, why are you persecuting *me*?" (Acts 9:4, emphasis added). Saul was not literally persecuting Jesus. Jesus had already ascended to heaven. He was already out of reach of Saul's hostility. Saul was busy persecuting Christians. But Jesus felt such solidarity with His church that He regarded an attack on His body, the church, as an attack on Himself.

The church is not Christ. Christ is perfect; the church is imperfect. Christ is the Redeemer; the church is the company of the redeemed. But the church belongs to Christ. The church is redeemed by Christ. The church is the bride of Christ. The church is indwelt by Christ.

In light of this solidarity, the church participates in Christ's suffering. But this participation adds nothing to Christ's merit. The sufferings of Christians may benefit other people, but they always fall short of atonement.

What is lacking in the afflictions of Jesus is the ongoing suffering that God calls His people to endure. God calls people of every generation to suffer.

We are followers of Christ. We follow Him to the garden of Gethsemane. We follow Him into the hall of judgment. We follow Him along the *Via Dolorosa*. We follow Him unto death. But the gospel declares that we also follow Him through the gates of heaven. Because we suffer with Him, we will also be raised with Him. If we are humiliated with Him, we will also be exalted with Him.

Because of Christ, our suffering is not useless. It is part of the total plan of God, who has chosen to redeem the world through the pathway of suffering.

Chapter Five

A Case Study in Suffering

The vice president of operations of a large corporation became intensely envious of a district manager in the company. The district manager enjoyed a close personal relationship with the chairman of the board. Moved by his envy, the vice president lodged a complaint with the chairman.

"I think we ought to get rid of Joe Hawkins," he suggested.

"Why?" the chairman asked. "He's one of our most productive managers. I think he's doing an outstanding job. And besides, he is the most loyal employee we have."

"Loyal? You think he's loyal?" the vice president said with dripping cynicism. "He's loyal only because you pay him such a high salary. You give him benefits that no one else receives. Besides, you've built a wall of protection around him. I wonder how loyal he'd be if you put the heat on him. Cut his salary and benefits; then see how loyal he is."

The chairman was irritated by this suggestion, but he responded to the challenge. "All right," he said. "Let's see about it. Go ahead and cut his salary. Put some heat on. I think you'll see that Hawkins will maintain his loyalty."

The vice president gave a sarcastic laugh. "You just let me at him and he'll betray you and the company in a minute."

The vice president left the boardroom and put together a scheme to bring Joe crashing down. First he cut his salary in half and canceled his health insurance. Then he approached some of Joe's coworkers and enlisted them in his scheme. They were eager to join in. They gleefully contrived plans of industrial sabotage to destroy Joe's productivity record. They falsified reports and covertly disrupted some of the machinery in the plant. Suddenly, Joe's plant was besieged with customer complaints about poor quality.

The pressure was on, but Joe took it in stride. He worked hard to solve the mysterious rash of problems that had arisen. This merely fueled the antagonism of his enemies. They began to put more pressure on. "Accidents" began to happen in the plant. The conspirators even started to harass Joe's family. To make matters worse, Joe suddenly became ill. The vice president had bribed a corrupt physician to introduce a virulent strain of bacteria into Joe's food.

Joe's world began to fall apart. His sickness took its toll. Coupled with the plunging productivity of his plant, his star began to fade.

Some of his closest friends came to him with sharp criticism. "What's wrong with you, Hawkins?" they asked. "You've lost something. Your performance is down. No wonder they cut your salary."

Joe's friends began to think that their former opinion of him had been wrong. They assumed that Joe must have done something really bad for his life to have taken such a sudden and drastic turn for the worse. One of his friends even came to him with "spiritual" counsel. "Joe," he said, "I need to tell you something in love. The troubles you've been having must come from God. I think it is all a kind of punishment for unconfessed sin in your life. Maybe if you repent, things will start to go better for you."

"Maybe you're right," Joe replied. "I'm not aware of anything I've done to deserve this, but I will certainly search my soul about it."

"But the chairman cut your salary in half. Doesn't that tell you something?"

"Well, the chairman has a right to do that. He has always been fair with me. I'm sure he knows what he is doing. He must have a good reason for his action," Joe answered.

Then Joe's wife got into the act. "Honey," she said one evening, "I think it's time for you to resign. Your health is failing and the company is treating you like dirt. After all your years of faithful service, this is the thanks you get. Let's get out and start over somewhere else. You're crazy to keep working for a company like this."

"No," Joe answered. "I can't leave."

"Why not?" his wife demanded.

"I owe it to the chairman of the board to stay on."

"Are you crazy? You don't owe him anything. You've given him the best years of your life, and now this. He owes *you*! You don't owe him a thing. Why don't you face it, Joe; the chairman's as rotten as the deal he has given you."

"No!" Joe snapped in anger. "I just can't believe that he would treat me unfairly on purpose."

"Then you'd better talk to him face-to-face. I'd love to hear what he will say if you confront him."

"OK, I'll talk to him," Joe promised.

The next day, Joe made an appointment to see the chairman. When he was ushered into the wood-paneled office, the chairman greeted him in a friendly manner. "Hi, Joe. What can I do for you?"

Joe got straight to the point. He gushed out his grievances in a torrent of rage. "What's going on here?" he demanded. "You've cut my salary in half. You stand by and let a bunch of thieves sabotage my plant. You've taken away my health benefits. What did I do to deserve this kind of treatment? I've been loyal to you and to the company for years, and now you treat me like this! Who do you think you are, anyway?"

The chairman listened patiently to Joe's diatribe. Then he responded. "Let me ask you some questions, Joe," he said. "Do you own this company?"

"No, sir," Joe replied.

"Did you build this place from scratch? Did you risk your own capital in this operation? Do you make payroll twice a month? Are you the chairman of the board?"

To all these questions, Joe shook his head.

"Tell me, Joe, who are you to tell me how to run my company? I've given you everything I ever promised you and more. Look at your contract. Does your contract specify that you should receive all the bonuses I've given you over the years?"

Again, Joe had to give an honest answer. "No, sir, you really have been more than kind to me."

"You say that I've been more than kind. Do you think I've changed? Do you think I'm not aware of what's been going on recently? I know exactly what's going on in your plant. I've been following the matter closely. Nothing has escaped my notice.

"Joe, I'm going to ask you to do something for me. You've trusted me in the past. Trust me now. I guarantee you that I will straighten things out. I have a plan. Those who have plotted against you will get everything they deserve. Do you really think I would let them get away with this?"

Joe felt awful. He began to stammer an apology. "I'm sorry," he said. "I had no right to come in here and lay all these accusations on you. I've complained once, but no more. You'll never hear another word of protest out of my mouth. Do whatever you will. I trust you."

The chairman smiled. Then he spoke into the intercom to his secretary. "Ms. Franklin," he said, "have the vice president of operations report to my office immediately.

"Don't leave yet, Joe. I have a few final words for you. First, I want you to know that when the vice president of operations gets here, I'm going to give him his walking papers. Beginning tomorrow morning, you will be the vice president of operations. You will receive double the salary you had before your pay was cut. I'm restoring your health benefits. And I have located a specialist who can treat and cure your disease.

"You have been loyal to me, Joe, more loyal than any other employee. You've endured a lot without cursing me behind my back. Now it is time for you to be vindicated."

"I knew it!" Joe exclaimed. "I had my moments of doubt, but deep down inside I knew you would fix everything. Now I really feel embarrassed for all those accusations I made to you. How can you ever forgive me?"

"Joe, don't worry about it. That's one thing I know how to do—forgive. I major in forgiveness."

By now you've probably recognized that this is the story of the biblical character Job, thinly disguised in modern terminology. The story of Job is a case study in human suffering. It chronicles the drama of a righteous man who underwent extreme misery in this world. His misery was compounded by his friends' insensitivity toward him. They made an assumption that the Bible forbids. They assumed that Job's degree of suffering was in direct proportion to his sin. They assumed that there is a ratio in our lives between suffering and guilt. Since Job's suffering was great, it must have been a sign that his sin was equally great.

God does not allow this equation. Jesus was questioned about the man who had been born blind: "As he passed by, he saw a man blind from birth. And his disciples asked him, 'Rabbi, who sinned, this man or his parents, that he was born blind?' Jesus answered, 'It was not that this man sinned, or his parents, but that the works of God might be displayed in him'" (John 9:1–3).

The fallacy of the false dilemma occurs when a problem is presented as though there were only two possible explanations, when in reality there may be three or more options. Some issues are indeed of an either/or character. For example, either there is a God or there is not. There is no third option. But because *some* questions may be reduced to only two alternatives does not mean that *all* questions may be so reduced.

This is the error that the disciples made concerning the man born blind. They assumed that there were only two possible explanations for the man's situation. The blindness was either the result of the man's sin or the result of his parents' sin.

Their thinking was wrong, but it was not utterly groundless. They were correct in one assumption. They knew enough about Scripture to realize that there is a connection between suffering and sin. They understood that suffering and death had entered the world because of sin. Before sin entered the world, there was no suffering or death.

Death is unnatural. It may be natural to fallen man, but it was not natural to man as he was created. Man was not created to die. He was created with the possibility of death, but not with the necessity of death. Death was introduced as a consequence of sin. If there had been no sin, there would be no death. But when sin entered, the curse of the fall was added.

The disciples were partially correct at another point. They were aware that sometimes there is a direct link between a person's sin and his suffering. For instance, God afflicted Miriam with leprosy as a judgment for her sin against Moses (Num. 12:9–10).

The error of the disciples was in their assumption that there is *always* a direct correspondence between a person's sin and his suffering. In this world, some people suffer far less than they deserve for their sins, while others endure a greater proportion of suffering. This disparity is seen in David's cry, "O LORD, how long shall the wicked, how long shall the wicked exult?" (Ps. 94:3).

There are times when we suffer innocently at other people's hands. When that occurs, we are victims of injustice. But that injustice happens on a horizontal plane. No one ever suffers injustice on the vertical plane. No one ever suffers unjustly in terms of his or her relationship with God. As long as we bear the guilt of sin, we cannot protest that God is unjust in allowing us to suffer.

Regardless, the disciples still committed the fallacy of the false dilemma. Jesus exposed their fallacy by saying, "Neither!" The reason that the man had been born blind was not his sin or his parents' sin. Jesus declared that the man had been born blind so "that the works of God might be displayed in him." The man born blind had been afflicted with blindness for the glory of God. This startling truth is a crucial teaching for us. It serves as a warning for us not to jump to conclusions about the "why" of our suffering.

God used the man's blindness for His greater glory. In this case, the "evil" of disease and suffering was made serviceable to God. He triumphed over it and brought His glorious plan to pass through it.

Likewise, in the dreadful suffering of Joseph at the hands of his brothers, the plan of God for all of history was brought to pass. After Joseph's reconciliation with his brothers, he exclaimed, "You meant evil against me, but God meant it for good, to bring it about that many people should be kept alive, as they are today" (Gen. 50:20).

God works through evil to accomplish salvation. God's working did not make the evil of Joseph's brothers any less evil. In the same way, Judas' betrayal of Jesus was a wicked act. It brought unjust suffering on Jesus, even as Joseph was a victim of his brothers' injustice. God does not create fresh evil in people's hearts; their evil acts arise out of their own sinful natures. Yet God has ordained to use that evil for His good purposes. Above all injustice, all pain, and all suffering stands a sovereign God who works His plan of salvation *over*, *against*, and even *through* evil.

What Jesus declared to His disciples about the blind man is clearly displayed in the book of Job. Had the disciples mastered this Old Testament book, perhaps they would not have fallen into the either/or fallacy. They made the same mistake committed by Job's friends.

Job protested the words of his friends. His reply is poignant: "I have heard many such things; miserable comforters are you all. Shall windy words have an end? Or what provokes you that you answer? I also could speak as you do, if you were in my place; I could join words together against you and shake my head at you. I could strengthen you with my mouth, and the solace of my lips would assuage your pain" (Job 16:2–5).

Consider the advice that Job received from his wife: "And he took a piece of broken pottery with which to scrape himself while he sat in the ashes. Then his wife said to him, 'Do you still hold fast your integrity? Curse God and die.' But he said to her, 'You speak as one of the foolish women would speak. Shall we receive good from God, and shall we not receive evil?' In all this Job did not sin with his lips" (Job 2:8–10).

One of the most difficult challenges a person faces in the midst of suffering is to receive well-intentioned counsel to give up the struggle. This counsel usually comes from those who are closest to us and who love us the most, as we saw when we considered Peter's rebuke in the previous chapter.

Job's wife told him, "Curse God and die." She encouraged him to compromise his integrity to alleviate his pain. She meant well. She obviously had compassion for her husband. She encouraged him to take the easy way out. But her words served only to increase Job's frustration. Job did not understand why God had called him to suffer, but he did understand that God *had* called him to suffer. It was hard enough for him to be faithful to his vocation without his loved ones' trying to talk him out of it.

At the nadir of his agony, Job declared, "Though he slay me, I will hope in him" (Job 13:15). Job's trust wavered, but it never died. He mourned. He cried. He protested. He questioned. He even cursed the day of his birth. But he clutched tightly to his only possible hope, his trust in God. At times, Job was hanging on by his fingernails. But he hung on. He cursed himself. He rebuked his wife. But he never cursed God.

Job cried out to God for answers to his questions. He desperately wanted to know why he had been called to endure so much suffering. Finally, God answered him out of the whirlwind. But the answer was not what Job had expected. God refused to grant Job a detailed explanation of His reasons for the affliction. God did not disclose His secret counsel to Job.

Ultimately the only answer that God gave to Job was a revelation of Himself. It was as though God said to him, "Job, *I* am your answer." Job was asked to trust not a plan but a person, a personal God who is sovereign, wise, and good. It was as though God said to Job: "Learn who I am. When you know Me, you know enough to handle anything."

God was asking Job to exercise an implicit faith. An implicit faith is not blind faith. It is a faith with vision, a vision enlightened by a knowledge of the character of God. If God never revealed anything about Himself to us and required us to trust Him in this darkness, the requirement would be for blind faith. We would be asked to make a blind leap of faith into the awful abyss of darkness.

But God never requires such foolish leaps. He never calls us to jump into the darkness. On the contrary, He calls us to forsake the darkness and enter the light. It is the light of His countenance. It is the radiant light of His person, which has no shadow of turning. When we are bathed in the refulgent splendor of the glory of His person, trust is not blind.

When Job declared, "Though he slay me, I will hope in him," he was revealing to us that though his knowledge of God was limited, it was still profound. He knew enough about the character of God to know that God was (and would always be) trustworthy.

God deserves to be trusted. The more we understand of His perfections, the more we understand how trustworthy He is. That is why the Christian pilgrimage moves from faith to faith, from strength to strength, and from grace to grace. Ironically, the progress passes through suffering and tribulation. That is why Paul could write these words: "Not only that, but we rejoice in our sufferings, knowing that suffering produces endurance, and endurance produces character, and character produces hope, and hope does not put us to shame, because God's love has been poured into our hearts through the Holy Spirit who has been given to us" (Rom. 5:3–5).

Here we are told that "hope does not put us to shame." Other translations speak of a hope that does not disappoint us. Blind hope, like blind faith, will indeed disappoint us.

Blind hope gropes aimlessly in the darkness. It stumbles over unseen obstacles. To put all of one's hope into a single goal and to have that goal unfulfilled is to be disappointed.

Hope that is blind can be embarrassing. We stick our necks out only to be left in disgrace if our boldness is not vindicated. But the hope that rests in Christ will not lead to embarrassment. The shame will be on those who put their hope in something else. The hope that fails is the hope that has no power to overcome suffering.

It is the hope of Christ that makes it possible for us to persevere in times of tribulation and distress. We have an anchor for our souls that rests in the One who has gone before us and conquered.

Chapter Six

Purpose in Suffering

A theological undercurrent runs through the book of Ecclesiastes and breaks through again and again. We see it when Solomon affirms that "for everything there is a season, and a time for every matter under heaven: a time to be born, and a time to die" (Eccl. 3:1–2), but it appears elsewhere, too. Solomon writes: "I perceived that whatever God does endures forever; nothing can be added to it, nor anything taken from it" (3:14); "Consider the work of God: who can make straight what he has made crooked?"

(7:13); and "All this I laid to heart, examining it all, how the righteous and the wise and their deeds are in the hand of God" (9:1). This theological undercurrent, which is found not just in Ecclesiastes but in the whole Old Testament and indeed in all of Scripture, is this: God ordains everything according to His purposes. In other words, God is sovereign.

I have never met a professing Christian who said that he did not believe in the sovereignty of God. We have an intuitive understanding that if God is God, He *must* be sovereign. It is impossible for God not to be sovereign, and any conception of a god that is less than sovereign is an idol and no god at all. So it is easy for believers to say, "I believe in the sovereignty of God," and we all affirm it—on the surface.

Yet the sovereignty of God is one of the most difficult doctrines to get into one's bloodstream and into the fiber of daily living, so that we live life believing that God is in fact sovereign and maintain our trust in Him even when it seems that life is spinning out of control. A great part of the difficulty we face in terms of accepting this doctrine stems from the presence of suffering in our lives. We say that we believe that God is sovereign, but when we wrestle with events in our own lives that are troublesome, bad things that happen to us, tragedies that befall us, we begin to question either the sovereignty of God or the goodness of God. Many of the theologies that flourish in our land are designed to sidestep that problem. They seek to absolve God from any responsibility for the tragedies of human life and to turn the ultimate sovereignty over to the human heart.

We have already seen that our suffering is part of the total plan of God and that God can work through evil to accomplish His plan. The fact that God has a plan indicates that He has a purpose. The fact that He is sovereign indicates that He is fulfilling that purpose even when He allows suffering to come upon us. As in the case of Job, He may not reveal what His purpose is, but we have good reason to trust Him.

The seventh chapter of Ecclesiastes gives us some interesting insights on this topic. The beginning of the chapter contains a series of aphorisms. It begins with these words: "A good name is better than precious ointment" (v. 1). In the ancient world, an ointment that relieved pain and suffering was very difficult to find or acquire, so it was seen as extremely valuable. But Solomon points out that a good name is even better than precious ointment. It is a very valuable thing.

Then he goes on to say, "And the day of death [is better] than the day of birth." This could be taken in a pessimistic way or from a transcendent viewpoint. So often in the Old Testament, we find people who are on the rim of despair, cursing the day they were born. When a person looks at life from the perspective of this world, sometimes he gets tired of living.

Ecclesiastes affirms that the day of a person's death is better than the day of his birth. That would be true for the pessimist, who can't wait to get it over with—at least if he only passes into oblivion rather than eternal punishment. But this sentiment is also true for the optimist, for the Christian. The day of one's birth is a good day for the believer, but the day of death is the greatest day that a Christian can ever experience in this world because that is the day he goes home, the day he walks across the threshold, the day he enters the Father's house. That is the day of ultimate triumph for the Christian in this world, and yet it is a day we fear and a day we postpone as long as we possibly can because we don't *really* believe that the day of our death is better than the day of our birth.

In Ecclesiastes 7:2–3, Solomon gives us a strange contrast: "It is better to go to the house of mourning than to go to the house of feasting, for this is the end of all mankind, and the living will lay it to heart. Sorrow is better than laughter, for by sadness of face the heart is made glad." The distinction here is one that is common to wisdom literature. It is the contrast between the wise and the fool. We may go to the house of mirth, to a party, where we have fun, kick back, have a good time, and enjoy entertainment. Parties are not too serious; we don't have to be contemplative to enjoy ourselves there. But how much do we learn in those circumstances? Times of mirth do very little for the good of our souls.

When we go to the house of mourning, however, we go to an environment where our hearts can be equipped with transcendent wisdom. It sometimes seems that only when suffering, pain, or grief invades our lives do we begin to be sober and direct our thinking toward the things of God in a significant way. The house of mourning has a way of prompting us to do that.

Certainly, Jesus was One who was often in the house of mourning. He was described as "a man of sorrows and acquainted with grief" (Isa. 53:3). Yet He spoke of His joy (John 15:11). For the Christian, there can be joy in the midst of suffering, joy that transcends the pain of the moment. But we don't really understand the grounds for this joy in the house of mirth. We discover it in the house of mourning. It is in weeping that we learn to contemplate the goodness of God. It is in mourning that we discover the peace of God that passes understanding.

Solomon goes on to say, "Sorrow is better than laughter." He doesn't mean that sorrow is good and laughter is bad. This is a comparison between the good and the better. It is better for us in the long run to experience sorrow than laughter. Why? Solomon gives us the answer: "For by sadness of face the heart is made glad. The heart of the wise is in the house of mourning, but the heart of fools is in the house of mirth" (Eccl. 7:3–4).

When we reach verse 13, we get a different perspective. Here Solomon writes, "Consider the work of God." Solomon challenges us not simply to observe God's work but to think deeply about it. We can observe His handiwork everywhere we look, but we need to do more than simply look at it—we need to consider it, to evaluate it, to seek its meaning, to arrive at some kind of understanding. We are to observe the work of God, that we might come to a better understanding of the character of God. We have to learn how to think theologically.

Solomon's next statement is a question that grows out of his own observation and consideration of God's work: "Who can make straight what he has made crooked?" This speaks to God's power and authority, His sovereignty. Then in verse 14, Solomon writes: "In the day of prosperity be joyful, and in the day of adversity consider: God has made the one as well as the other." The idea communicated here may be the best-kept secret of Christendom. It is an idea that speaks to the matter of the sovereignty of God. This call to consider the work of God is a call to examine not just creation but the work of God in history. This is a call to reflect on the providence of God, because He is the Author of all things mirthful *and* all things mournful.

We tend to be able to see the hand of divine providence in our lives when we pray earnestly for something and God says yes. When we want something desperately and pray about it intensely, and God answers no, what happens? We begin to doubt that there even is a God. So the no response from God is negative in our lives, whereas the yes response affirms our faith. Solomon is saying that if you want to be wise, you must consider both, because God's hand is as sovereign in the no as it is in the yes. God displays His providence as much in suffering as in prosperity.

The bottom line for anyone who believes in the God of providence is that ultimately there are no tragedies. God has promised that all things that happen in this world—all pain, all suffering, all tragedies—are but for a moment, and that He works in and through these events for the good of those who love Him. That's why the Apostle Paul said that the pain, the suffering, the affliction that we bear in this world isn't worthy to be compared with the glory and the blessedness that God has stored up for His people (Rom. 8:18).

Sometimes it seems that earlier generations of Christians had a higher view of God than we do. The reason for that may very well lie in that they were much more familiar with pain, with suffering, with persecution, and with death than we are. Because of all they endured, they were forced to consider the hand of God in the midst of their difficulties.

God's hand is in affliction. His sovereignty is manifest in the dark side of life. This is said so frequently in Scripture that it is amazing how hard it is for us to grasp it. We tend to shut our minds off from thinking about these things. Why do we go to the house of mirth in the first place? For many of us, a party is not simply an opportunity to have a good time but a chance to get away from thinking. We look for an escape, an avenue of pleasure that will somehow dull the fears and the aches that we carry about. But the wise person looks for the finger of God in the house of mourning as well as in the house of mirth—in all things that take place.

It is interesting to consider how Solomon begins chapter 8 of Ecclesiastes. Having just affirmed these difficult truths regarding God's sovereignty, he writes: "Who is like the wise? And who knows the interpretation of a thing? A man's wisdom makes his face shine, and the hardness of his face is changed" (v. 1). After hearing Solomon tell us that it is better to go to the house of mourning than to the house of mirth, we might get the idea that God wants His people to be so contemplative that they walk around stone-faced, with a dour disposition. That is not at all what the author of Ecclesiastes intends. He is affirming that when we understand the sovereignty of God, it changes our countenance. It changes our demeanor. Those who understand God's sovereignty have joy even in the midst of suffering, a joy reflected on their very faces, for they see that their suffering is not without purpose.

Chapter Seven

The Final Calling

We have considered suffering as a vocation. Dare we think of death as a vocation, too?

The author of Ecclesiastes made this declaration: "For everything there is a season, and a time for every matter under heaven: a time to be born, and a time to die" (Eccl. 3:1–2). Likewise, the author of Hebrews says, "It is appointed for man to die once, and after that comes judgment" (Heb. 9:27).

Notice the language of Scripture. It speaks of death in terms of a "season" and a "time" under heaven. Death is a divine appointment. It is part of God's purpose for our lives. God calls each person to die. He is sovereign over all of life, including the final experience of life.

We usually limit the idea of vocation to our careers or our jobs. The word *vocation*, however, comes from the Latin word *vocare*, meaning "to call." Used in the Christian sense, *vocation* refers to a divine calling, a summons that comes from God Himself. He calls people to teach, to preach, to sing, to make cars, and to change diapers. There are as many vocations as there are facets to human life.

We have different vocations with respect to the jobs and tasks that God gives us in this life. But we all share in the vocation of death. Every one of us is called to die. That vocation is as much a calling from God as is a "call" to the ministry of Christ. Sometimes the call comes suddenly and without warning. Sometimes it comes with advance notice. But it comes to all of us. And it comes from God.

There are teachers who tell us that God has nothing to do with death. Death is seen strictly as a fiendish device of the devil. All pain, suffering, disease, and tragedy are blamed on the evil one. God is absolved of any responsibility. This view is designed to make sure that God is free of blame for anything that goes wrong in this world. "God always wills healing," we are told. If that healing does not happen, then the fault lies with Satan—or with us. Death, they say, is not in the plan of God. It represents a victory for Satan over the realm of God.

Such views may bring temporary relief to the afflicted. But they are not true. They have nothing to do with biblical Christianity. They are intended to absolve God of any blame, but they contradict His sovereignty.

Yes, there is a devil. He is our archenemy. He will do anything in his power to bring misery into our lives. But Satan is not sovereign. Satan does not hold the keys of death.

When Jesus appeared in a vision to the Apostle John on the Isle of Patmos, He identified Himself with these words: "Fear not, I am the first and the last, and the living one. I died, and behold I am alive forevermore, and I have the keys of Death and Hades" (Rev. 1:17–18).

Jesus holds the keys to death, and Satan cannot snatch those keys out of His hand. Christ's grip is firm. He holds the keys because He owns the keys. All authority in heaven and on earth has been given to Him. That includes all authority over life and death. The angel of death is at His beck and call.

World history has witnessed the emergence of many forms of religious dualism. Dualism affirms the existence of two equal and opposite forces. These forces are variously called good and evil, God and Satan, yin and yang. The two forces are locked in eternal combat. Since they are equal as well as opposite, the conflict goes on forever, with neither side ever gaining the upper hand. The world is doomed to serve as the eternal battleground between these hostile forces. We are the victims of their struggle, the pawns in their eternal chess game.

Dualism is on a collision course with Christianity. The Christian faith has no stock in dualism. Satan may be *opposed* to God, but he is by no means *equal* to God. Satan is a creature; God is the Creator. Satan is potent; God is omnipotent. Satan is knowledgeable and crafty; God is omniscient. Satan is localized in his presence; God is omnipresent. Satan is finite; God is infinite. The list could go on. But it is clear from Scripture that Satan is not an ultimate force in any sense.

We are not doomed to an ultimate conflict with no hope of resolution. The message of Scripture is one of victory—full, final, and ultimate victory. It is not our doom that is certain, but Satan's. His head has been crushed by the heel of Christ, who is the Alpha and Omega.

Above all suffering and death stands the crucified and risen Lord. He has defeated the ultimate enemy of life. He has vanquished the power of death. He calls us to die, a call to obedience in the final transition of life. Because of Christ, death is not final. It is a passage from one world to the next.

God does not always will healing. If He did, He would suffer endless frustration, seeing His will being repeatedly thwarted in the deaths of His people. He did not will the healing of Stephen from the wounds inflicted by the stones that were hurled against him. He did not will the healing of Moses, Joseph, David, Paul, Augustine, Martin Luther, or John Calvin. These all died in faith. Ultimate healing comes through death and after death.

Teachers argue that there is healing in the atonement of Christ. Indeed there is. Jesus bore all our sins on the cross. Yet none of us is free from sin in this life. Likewise, none of us is free from sickness in this life. The healing that is in the cross is real. We participate in its benefits now, in this life. But the fullness of the healing from both sin and disease takes place in heaven. We must still die at our appointed times.

When God issues a call to us, it is always a holy call. The vocation of dying is a sacred vocation. To understand that is one of the most important lessons a Christian can ever learn. When the summons comes, we can respond in many ways. We can become angry, bitter, or terrified, but if we see it as a call from God and not a threat from Satan, we are far more prepared to cope with its difficulties.

When God gives us a vocation to die, He sends us on a mission. The course may be frightening. It is an obstacle course with pitfalls along the way. We wonder whether we will have the courage to make our way to the finish line, for the trail takes us through the valley of shadows.

The valley of the shadow of death is a place where the sun's rays often seem to be blotted out. To approach it is to tremble. We would prefer to walk around it, to seek a safe bypass. But men and women of faith can enter that valley without fear. David told us how: "Even though I walk through the valley of the shadow of death, I will fear no evil, for you are with me; your rod and your staff, they comfort me" (Ps. 23:4).

David was a shepherd. In this psalm, David put himself in the place of the sheep. He saw himself as a lamb under the care of the Great Shepherd. He entered the valley without fear for one ultimate reason—the Shepherd went with him. He trusted himself to the care and the protection of the Shepherd.

The lamb found comfort in the Shepherd's tools, the rod and the staff. The ancient shepherd was armed. He could use the crook of his staff to rescue a fallen lamb from a pit. He could wield his rod against hostile beasts that sought to devour his sheep. Without the shepherd, the sheep would have been helpless in the shadowy valley. But as long as the shepherd was present, the sheep had nothing to fear.

If a bear or lion attacked and killed the shepherd, the sheep would scatter. They would be vulnerable to the lion's jaws. If the shepherd fell, all was lost for the sheep.

But we have a Shepherd who *cannot* fall and who *will not* abandon His flock at the first sign of trouble. Our Shepherd is armed with omnipotent force. He is not threatened by the valley of shadows. He is Lord of the valley.

David's confidence was rooted in the absolute certainty of the presence of God. He understood that with a divine vocation comes divine assistance and the absolute promise of the divine presence. God will not send us where He refuses to go Himself.

God is our refuge and our strength in times of trouble. His promise is not only that He will go with us into the valley. Even more important is His promise of what lies on the other side of the valley. God promises to go with us for the entire journey in order to guide us to what lies beyond. The valley of the shadow of death is not a box canyon. It is a passageway to a better country. The valley leads to life—life far more abundant than anything we can imagine. The goal of the vocation of death is heaven itself. But there is no route to heaven except through this valley.

David also understood that. Though he lived before Christ, before the resurrection, before the New Testament revelation of glory, nevertheless God had not been altogether silent on the matter. Already there was the hope of "Abraham's side" (Luke 16:22).

David confessed his faith in this manner: "I would have lost heart, unless I had believed that I would see the goodness of the Lord in the land of the living" (Ps. 27:13, NKJV).

The God of Abraham, Isaac, and Jacob is the God of the living. The God of David is the God of the living. The God of Jesus is the God of the living. There is life beyond the shadow of death.

Chapter Eight

Dying in Faith

The question that plagues us about death is not *whether* we will die. A macabre saying holds that there are only two certain things in life—death and taxes. But some people manage to avoid or evade taxes. The only way that we can possibly avoid death is to remain alive until the return of Christ.

I just had to change the words of the previous sentence. At first I wrote these words: "The only way that we can possibly avoid death is to *be alive at* the return of Christ."

I changed the wording because my original sentence was at least misleading and at worst heretical. The New Testament assures us that all who are in Christ will certainly be alive at His coming. If we die before He returns, we will be raised to witness His glorious return:

> But we do not want you to be uninformed, brothers, about those who are asleep, that you may not grieve as others do who have no hope. For since we believe that Jesus died and rose again, even so, through Jesus, God will bring with him those who have fallen asleep. For this we declare to you by a word from the Lord, that we who are alive, who are left until the coming of the Lord, will not precede those who have fallen asleep. For the Lord himself will descend from heaven with a cry of command, with the voice of an archangel, and with the sound of the trumpet of God. And the dead in Christ will rise first. Then we who are alive, who are left, will be caught up together with them in the clouds to meet the Lord in the air, and so we will always be with the Lord. Therefore encourage one another with these words. (1 Thess. 4:13–18)

Here the Apostle Paul gives a vivid description of what is popularly called the rapture of the saints. No Christian will miss the rapture. Those who remain alive until it happens will have no advantage over those who have already died. The dead in Christ will be raised for this event.

None of us saw the birth of Christ. We missed His dazzling display of miracles during His earthly ministry. Likewise, nobody alive today beheld Christ's agony on the cross. None of us was an eyewitness of His glorious resurrection and ascension into heaven. But no Christian will sleep through the second coming of Christ. Though we did not see His first coming, we will all be eyewitnesses of His return. The climax of the exaltation of Jesus will be viewed by every believer. God will raise the dead to make certain that every eye will behold His triumphant return.

We have many questions about our own deaths. We wonder *where* we will die. We ponder *when* we will die. We ask *why* we will die. The chief concern of Scripture, however, is *how* we will die. No, the Bible does not deal with specific causes of death. We know that we can die of cancer, from a heart attack, from violence on the part of another, from an accident, or from one of a host of other mortal causes. But these causes of biological death are not the chief concern of Scripture.

When Scripture speaks of the *how* of death, the focus is on the spiritual state of the person at the time of his death. Here we see the *how* of death reduced to only two options. Either we die in faith or we die in our sins:

> "Son of man, I have made you a watchman for the house of Israel. Whenever you hear a word from my mouth, you shall give them warning from me. If I say to the wicked, 'You shall surely die,' and you give him no warning, nor speak to warn the wicked from his wicked way, in order to save his life, that wicked person shall die for his iniquity, but his blood I will require at your hand. But if you warn the wicked, and he does not turn from his wickedness, or from his wicked way, he shall die for his iniquity, but you will have delivered your soul." (Ezek. 3:17–19)

What Ezekiel declared in the Old Testament, Jesus reaffirmed in the New Testament: "I told you that you would die in your sins, for unless you believe that I am he you will die in your sins" (John 8:24).

We sometimes think that the worst thing that can befall a person is to die. That is not the message of Jesus. According to Christ, the worst possible thing that can befall us is to die in our sins.

This is the biblical message that is so widely ignored in our day. We like to believe that everyone who dies automatically goes to heaven. We assume that the only ticket required for entrance into the kingdom of God is death. The warning required by Ezekiel is ignored because we do not believe that it is necessary.

Speaking to a dying person about his need for a Savior is not an easy matter. The last thing we want to do to a person in such a condition is to disturb him in any way or to make him feel uncomfortable. We naturally think that it is an act of human kindness not to discuss such matters. But God commands us to speak to the dying about their need for a Savior. Ezekiel makes that crystal clear. If we love people, we will warn them of the consequences of dying in their sins.

Jeremiah complained before God because God had called him to give the people a warning that they did not want to hear. To make matters worse for Jeremiah, his ministry was being undermined by false prophets who were very popular because they told the people what they wanted to hear. They promised, "Peace, peace," when there was no peace (Jer. 8:11).

Speaking for God, Jeremiah declared: "Do not listen to the words of the prophets who prophesy to you, filling you with vain hopes. They speak visions of their own minds, not from the mouth of the LORD. They say continually to those who despise the word of the LORD, 'It shall be well with you'; and to everyone who stubbornly follows his own heart, they say, 'No disaster shall come upon you'" (Jer. 23:16–17).

The message of the false prophets served only to heal the hurts of the people *slightly* (Jer. 8:11). False words of comfort are like putting a bandage on a gaping wound. The healing is at best slight. The false prophets were giving a crude form of slight relief instead of the authentic balm of Gilead.

The great lie is the one that declares that there is no last judgment. Yet if Jesus of Nazareth taught anything, He emphatically taught that there would be a last judgment. We do not respect Jesus as a teacher if we ignore His instruction on this matter. Consider these words of Christ:

> "When the Son of Man comes in his glory, and all the angels with him, then he will sit on his glorious

> throne. Before him will be gathered all the nations, and he will separate people one from another as a shepherd separates the sheep from the goats. And he will place the sheep on his right, but the goats on the left. Then the King will say to those on his right, 'Come, you who are blessed by my Father, inherit the kingdom prepared for you from the foundation of the world.' . . .
>
> "Then he will say to those on his left, 'Depart from me, you cursed, into the eternal fire prepared for the devil and his angels.' . . . And these will go away into eternal punishment, but the righteous into eternal life." (Matt. 25:31–34, 41, 46)

Here Jesus uttered sober words of warning. Those who die in their sins will be separated; they will be numbered with the goats.

Jesus amplified this warning elsewhere. He warned that "nothing is hidden that will not be made manifest, nor is anything secret that will not be known and come to light" (Luke 8:17). He also said: "Nothing is covered up that will not be revealed, or hidden that will not be known. Therefore whatever you have said in the dark shall be heard in the light, and what you have whispered in private rooms shall be proclaimed on the housetops" (12:2–3).

Jesus warned that a day will come when all secrets will become known. It will be the final end to all the cover-ups of this world. Every closet will be opened and the skeletons will be made plainly visible. The sins of us all will be made known unless we are "covered" by the cloak of Christ's righteousness.

This future day of nakedness is a day when those who die in their sins will "say to the mountains, 'Fall on us,' and to the hills, 'Cover us'" (Luke 23:30).

The New Testament describes Jesus as "Savior." The name *Jesus* was announced by the archangel Gabriel when he visited Mary. An angelic message to Joseph confirmed this name: "She will bear a son, and you shall call his name Jesus, for he will save his people from their sins" (Matt. 1:21).

The salvation of which the Bible speaks has a specific goal. The term *salvation* in general can be used for many things. Any type of rescue from danger or calamity can be called salvation. Biblically, a person can be saved from a disease or from financial disaster. If an army escapes defeat in battle, it experiences salvation.

But the salvation wrought by Jesus is not of this general type. It is specific. Jesus saves us "from the wrath to come" (1 Thess. 1:10).

The God of the Bible is a God of justice. His own character is just. Therefore, for God not to correct injustices in this world, to let the scales of justice remain forever out of balance, would be for Him to compromise His own integrity. This is precisely what He refuses to do. He promises ultimate justice.

The Judge of all the earth cannot bring forth final justice without a final judgment. He insists that all human beings will be held accountable for their actions. If we are not ultimately accountable, then the only conclusion we can reach is that ultimately we don't count. The bottom line would be that it doesn't ultimately matter how we live our lives, but every one of us knows that it *does* matter how people live.

Each one of us has been a victim of injustice at one point or another. Likewise, each one of us has committed injustices against other people. We experience and commit such injustice because, as sinners, we are unjust people.

The dilemma we face is this: God is just. We are unjust. This is the worst dilemma that a human being can face.

For a guilty person to face the justice meted out in our criminal justice system is one thing. To stand before the tribunal of God is something else. We cry out with David, "If you, O Lord, should mark iniquities, O Lord, who could stand?" (Ps. 130:3). David's question is rhetorical. The answer is obvious: *no one* will be able to stand.

The central issue of Christianity is the issue of justification. It faces the dilemma squarely. The only possible way for an unjust person to stand in the presence of a just and holy God is to be justified. If we remain unjustified, we die in our sins.

The only way that we can be justified is by the righteousness of Christ. He alone has the merit necessary to cover us. That righteousness is received by faith. If we trust in Christ, we are covered by His righteousness and are justified by faith. If we do not trust in Christ, we will stand before God's judgment alone, unjust people before a just God.

We suffer from two grand delusions. The first delusion is that we are good enough to stand in the presence of a perfectly righteous God. It is a delusion because every one of us has sinned. We have to be perfectly free of sin and perfectly righteous in order to stand before God. We are deluding ourselves in the extreme if we think that we are perfect.

Only a few people become deluded enough to think that they are without sin. This is not the delusion from which most of us suffer. It is the second delusion that catches so many of us. The fact that God is just and that we are unjust doesn't seem to bother us. We nurture the hope that since God is loving and merciful, He will make room for us in heaven even if we never repent of our sins and embrace Christ as Savior. We think that faith is not a necessary condition for salvation.

This delusion hurls an insult at the mercy of God. It assumes that by crucifying His only begotten Son for us, God did not do enough. It concludes that His requirements of faith and trust in the atoning Savior are a bit narrow.

The author of Hebrews labors to warn his readers of the consequences that flow from ignoring the priestly act of atonement rendered by Jesus. He raises another rhetorical question: "How shall we escape if we neglect such a great salvation? It was declared at first by the Lord, and it was attested to us by those who heard" (Heb. 2:3).

This warning is followed by further admonitions: "Take care, brothers, lest there be in any of you an evil, unbelieving heart, leading you to fall away from the living God. But exhort one another every day, as long as it is called 'today,' that none of you may be hardened by the deceitfulness of sin. . . . And to whom did he swear that they would not enter his rest, but to those who were disobedient? So we see that they were unable to enter because of unbelief" (3:12–13, 18–19).

The warning of Scripture stresses that as long as we delay repentance and faith, we run the risk of being "hardened" through the deceitfulness of sin. We've heard the gospel preached so often that we can become calloused to it. Our hearts can become calcified; our consciences can be seared. That is how sin works. First, we excuse ourselves and seek all manner of self-justification. Finally, we deceive ourselves into thinking that faith and repentance are not necessary.

God says that repentance and faith are necessary, utterly necessary. Hebrews declares that God is so serious about this that He swore a vow not to let the disobedient enter into His rest. Never was a more sacred oath sworn. It is the worst kind of delusion to even entertain the possibility that God will not keep this vow.

The author of Hebrews concludes by saying, "So we see that they were unable to enter because of unbelief" (v. 19). If a person remains in unbelief, it is simply not possible for him to enter the rest of God. Unbelief is a barrier to heaven.

We see, then, that there are only two ways of dying. We can die in faith or we can die in our sins. There are no second chances after death. The urgent focus of Scripture is on the necessity of repentance *before* we die. Again the author of Hebrews declares, "It is appointed for man to die once, and after that comes judgment" (9:27).

Just as God swore an oath that the impenitent will not enter His rest, so He swore that those who repent and believe in Christ *will* enter His rest. Again the author of Hebrews elaborates: "Therefore, while the promise of entering his rest still stands, let us fear lest any of you should seem to have failed to reach it. . . . For we who have believed enter that rest" (4:1, 3).

Hebrews 4 concludes with these words:

> Since then we have a great high priest who has passed through the heavens, Jesus, the Son of God, let us hold fast our confession. For we do not have a high priest who is unable to sympathize with our weaknesses, but one who in every respect has been tempted as we are, yet without sin. Let us then with

> confidence draw near to the throne of grace, that we may receive mercy and find grace to help in time of need. (vv. 14–16)

If we die in faith, we join a great assembly of those who have gone before us. Hebrews provides a litany of the heroes of faith who have died:

> By faith Abel offered to God a more acceptable sacrifice. . . . By faith Enoch was taken up. . . . By faith Noah, being warned by God concerning events as yet unseen, in reverent fear constructed an ark. . . .
>
> By faith Abraham obeyed when he was called to go out to a place that he was to receive as an inheritance. And he went out, not knowing where he was going. . . . By faith Sarah herself received power to conceive. . . .
>
> These all died in faith, not having received the things promised, but having seen them and greeted them from afar, and having acknowledged that they were strangers and exiles on the earth. For people who speak thus make it clear that they are seeking